Anonymous

# The Tehuantepec Ship Railway

Its Practicability and Commercial Features

Anonymous

**The Tehuantepec Ship Railway**
*Its Practicability and Commercial Features*

ISBN/EAN: 9783744726573

Printed in Europe, USA, Canada, Australia, Japan

Cover: Foto ©Suzi / pixelio.de

More available books at **www.hansebooks.com**

THE

# Tehuantepec Ship Railway;

ITS

## Practicability and Commercial Features.

---

*From* "THE MEXICAN FINANCIER,"
*December, 1884.*

---

NEW YORK:
BOWNE & CO., PRINTERS, 124 PEARL STREET.

1884.

# Tehuantepec Ship Railway,

DESIGNED TO TRANSPORT VESSELS OVERLAND BE-
TWEEN THE ATLANTIC AND PACIFIC OCEANS,
ACROSS THE ISTHMUS OF TEHUANTEPEC,
IN MEXICO.

---

In the discussion of this subject, we propose to show the commercial necessity, practicability, advantages, business and revenue of the TEHUANTEPEC SHIP RAILWAY.

## FIRST.

### COMMERCIAL NECESSITY.

The Rocky Mountains of the United States, the Sierra Madre of Mexico, the Cordilleras of Central America, and the Andes of South America form an almost continuous barrier, so lofty and extensive as to be nearly impassable to man in his commercial pursuits. The railways that scale these heights by an immense expenditure of money, seeking the business of the fertile valleys on each side, rise to an altitude of several thousand feet, soar up among the clouds, climb over the rocky barrier, and descend the mountain sides by grades almost impracticable for their heavily loaded trains. These mountain barriers separate at least seventy million people living in Mexico, the United States and Canada, nearly all of whom would be benefited by the breaking down of this obstruction to their agricultural, manufacturing and commercial prosperity.

The latest compilation of the internal commerce of the United States alone, shows an aggregate amount of over ten billions of dollars per annum; more than the value of all the foreign commerce of Great Britain, France, Germany, Russia, Holland, Austria and Belgium combined. This internal commerce is carried on through the network of her rivers, her extensive coast line and her railroads. The productions of the United States, of almost every kind, are becoming superabundant, requiring for the full extension and growth of its varied industries a commercial interchange with other nations lying to the east or to the west of her obstructing mountain ranges. The Pacific coast, with all its remarkable development of the past few years, now finds itself too far away from the markets of those nations which need its surplus productions. India and Australia are making strong efforts to supply the demand of those countries which the Pacific coast labors in vain to reach over a course of sixteen thousand miles around Cape Horn. The transcontinental railroad lines cannot afford to carry grain from Portland and San Francisco to New York for home consumption or transhipment to Liverpool. The producers and shippers alike look with anxious eyes to every project for breaking down the Isthmian barrier which now stands between them and the markets of the world, and places them four months away from their customers.

The Pacific coast is separated not only from the Atlantic and European ports, but from the eastern coast of South America and the West Indies, and especially from the Gulf ports of the United States, which are the natural entrepots and exporting centres of all the immense surplus productions of the great valley of the Mississippi. The value of the annual productions of the Mississippi Valley is estimated at nearly four billion dollars, and their natural outlet to the world is through the Gulf of Mexico, reaching it through the sixteen thousand miles of navigable rivers, trunk and branches of the Mississippi, seeking by water and rail the great commercial city of New Orleans, second to New York alone in the value of her exports. Here let it be said, that while opening to the world's commerce the valley of the Mississippi, by removing the barrier at the mouth of the River, Mr. JAMES B. EADS conceived the greater work of removing the more serious obstacle to commerce that, directly across the Gulf from the jetties at the mouth of the South Pass, rises up between the oceans and between the nations. Again, Galveston, the seaport city of Texas, (a State of two millions of inhabitants, with six thousand miles of railways) is still more completely isolated than New Orleans; with deep water secured for its harbor, it will need even more than at present a direct outlet for its commerce into the Pacific Ocean. Again, Boston, New York, Philadelphia, Baltimore and many intermediate ports and their tributary territory are excluded by the same barrier from all that lies west of these chains of mountains, not only the western coast of South America, as far south as Chili, and the western coast of Mexico, but the eastern coasts of the old world—Japan, China, India, Australasia, and the almost numberless Isles of the Pacific. The United States and Mexico need the surplus peculiar productions of these countries; they need our manufactured products; but the interchange can now be carried on only by transhipment and railroad carriage over the Panama Isthmus, at a cost of from ten to twenty-five dollars per ton of freight, and twenty-five dollars per head of passengers, or by the long, circuitous and dangerous passage around Cape Horn or the Cape of Good Hope, or the expensive route, via the Suez Canal.

Great Britain, the great carrier of the nations, whose flag floats over seventy per cent. of the world's marine, suffers from this barrier standing stolidly and forever between her and the commercial objects of her desire. This barrier is also an obstruction to the commerce of France and other maritime nations of Europe.

To sum up these general statements and to bring together these various features of the subject; the world needs a Gateway through the mountains, a path broad and plain for the intercommunication of the nations, on the shortest possible lines, for the transportation of the varied products which each nation has in surplus for the other's need. More than most other nations does the United States require that extension of her coast line from the east to the west, and the west to the east, which a navigable connection between the Gulf of Mexico and the Pacific, will give her. More vitally still, though the magnitude of the commerce is less, does the Republic of Mexico need a union of her east and west coast lines across the Isthmus of Tehuantepec, as an auxiliary to the extensive and necessary railway system which this young republic has so heroically inaugurated at great present sacrifice, but for the future greatness and prosperity to which her wonderful natural resources·entitle her. With the railroads, and the Ship Railway ; with abundant communication by land and by sea ; with the throbbings of a new strong national life, and with an internal and coastwise commerce of her own, she will eventually reach such a lofty position among the nations, that her statesmen will be proud of the great stride they have now taken in the march of the world's civilization, and her people will so devoutly reverence the greatness of their country, that no dissensions will be permitted to jeopardize its prosperity and growth.

The preceding general statement is but an epitome of the voluminous reports that have been made and the facts and arguments that have been given during the last three centuries, urging individuals and governments to undertake the removal of this barrier to commerce.

Said General J. G. Barnard, in a brief review of this subject several years ago : " No commercial, agricultural or speculative problem has had a history more marked. From the era of the Spanish conquest of America, the search for the secret of the supposed natural strait was carried on along the coast line of the two continents, and when this ceased, the possibility of the construction of an artificial route began to be discussed. During the last fifty years, governments, companies and individuals have devoted much time and money to the search for a practical route for ships."

Many independent surveys on different lines covering nearly the whole length of the American Isthmus, have been made during the last sixty-five years and embrace particularly the Panama, Nicaragua and Tehuantepec routes, the latter being the most northern and more than twelve hundred miles from the Panama route measured along the axis of the Isthmus.

The facts connected with the attempt to cut a ship canal through the Isthmus at Panama below the sea level, are too generally known to be referred to here, except to say that the impracticability of constructing the work for any sum of money commensurate with the probable revenue, was the reason for the inception of the Ship Railway and for a location more advantageous to commerce.

The location of the proposed Nicaragua Canal, lies north of Panama. Very elaborate surveys were made here by the United States Government, and a concession was granted by the Republic of Nicaragua to a ship canal company, but the terms of the concession not having been complied with it has recently been declared forfeited by that government.

At Tehuantepec, many surveys have been made by governments and individuals, looking to the construction of an ordinary railroad, a canal with locks and a Ship Railway. The advantages of this route as relates to commerce, climate, construction and maintenance, will be fully given under the appropriate subject. It is only necessary now to support these views of the commercial necessity for an inter-oceanic communication by the publicly expressed opinions of men capable of forming a correct judgment.

The views expressed by Secretary Marcy, Presidents Buchanan, Hayes, Garfield and Arthur, and Secretary Frelinghuysen, all confirm the opinions advanced that this commercial necessity exists.

One of the most far-seeing statesmen of this day who comprehends the immense commercial advantages to be gained by establishing an inter-oceanic communication between the Atlantic and Pacific, U. S. Senator William Windom, while calling attention to the map of the world in the Senate Chamber, in 1881, used the following expressive language :—

" Bordering upon the Gulf on the north lie the great States " of Texas, Louisiana, Mississippi, Alabama and Florida. " North of these lies the mighty empire drained by the Mis- " sissippi River, while to the east are the Atlantic States, " stretching from Florida to Maine. On the Pacific are the " States of California, Oregon and Washington Territory, and " from the Atlantic to the Pacific, stretches a domain whose " magnificence is the pride of every American. Obstructing,

"embarrassing and burdening the commerce between these
"great sections of the Union, lies this narrow strip of land.
"* * * * To avoid it, 1,200,000 tons of wheat raised in Cal-
"ifornia and Oregon last year are compelled to seek a Euro-
"pean market by a costly and tedious voyage of fourteen
"thousand miles around Cape Horn. Even the exchange of
"productions between our own Atlantic and Pacific States
"must be made by the same circuitous, expensive and dan-
"gerous route, or else sustain the heavy burdens imposed for
"railway transportation across the continent. The com-
"merce of all the leading nations is in like manner obstructed
"and burdened. The time has come when this barrier is to
"be removed. The wonder is that it has been permitted to
"remain so long."

Touching on some of the commercial results to be gained
by a crossing of the American isthmus for ships, General
Grant stated in the *North American Review* in 1881:—

"The States of North and South America, lying along the
"Pacific furnish in large abundance those commodities which
"are constantly needed in the markets of almost every country
"of Europe. Of guano and nitre the trade is immense. From
"the ports of Chili, nearly four hundred thousand tons of
"freight are shipped eastward annually. More than one
"million tons of grain are shipped each year from the Pacific
"States and Territories. There is, no doubt, that more than
"4,000,000 tons of merchandise find their way from the east
"and require water communication, in order that they may
"be shipped economically and profitably, and this is mer-
"chandise to which railway transportation across the conti-
"nent is wholly inapplicable."

The statesmen of Mexico from Hernando Cortez to the present time, have been fully aware of the immense benefit to
Mexico, that would inevitably result from an inter-oceanic
crossing at the Isthmus of Tehuantepec. Cortez himself
sought for it, and when his examinations showed no natural
opening through the mountains at the level of the sea or by
the rivers, his great mind looked forward into the distant
future, and he saw in imagination what is soon to be realized
—a commercial Gateway between the Oceans. Believing that

this isthmus would certainly become the route for commerce, he purchased extensive tracts of land for his posterity, who still possess them, and through which the Ship Railway route is located by the recent surveys. Three centuries have passed ; Mexico has passed through fire and sword to reach her present position among the nations. During all these years she has assisted by her means and by her wise counsel and official approval, every effort made to surmount the obstacles. She has, by her own able engineers, made careful surveys for canals and railroads ; she materially assisted by her means and by her engineers in the surveys for the Ship Railway, and placed at the head of the parties, that distinguished engineer, Don Francisco De Garay, Chief Engineer of the drainage of the valley of Mexico. But greater than all other aid has been the earnest support of the greatest statesman of the Mexico of to-day, General Porfirio Diaz. Grasping the situation, realizing the important and lasting benefits that would accrue to Mexico, he cordially and earnestly approved the proposition of Mr. Eads to construct a Ship Railway, as the final and complete solution of the problem of the centuries, and affixed his name with just pride to the official document that conceded to an American citizen the right to perform this great work.

There might be given here other weighty and valuable opinions from able men, but sufficient are given to show plainly that there is a necessity for a Ship Railway across the Isthmus of Tehuantepec—a necessity that affects the commerce of the world and its productions, agricultural, mineral and manufacturing. The removal of this obstruction will do as much towards uniting the world and bringing together in bonds of union, friendship and the peaceful arts of a christian civilization, the nations of the wide world, as any scheme of evangelization and civilization ever conceived. Shorten the distance between christendom and heathendom, and the subtile and ennobling influence of religion will, like the electric cable, unite all nations in the brotherhood of humanity. When this thought was presented to a prominent and wealthy railroad president, whose life-long desires go out to all the world for its christianization and civili-

zation, he said : "I have not considered fully the prac-
"ticability of the Ship Railway, but such a project,
"contemplating and, if successful, surely bringing about
"such important results in the grand work of elevating the
"human race, is worthy the help of all men." To prove the
sincerity of his expression he subscribed liberally towards the
expenses of the preliminary work. A few days ago he saw
the Ship Railway Model, which presents in a concrete form the
methods proposed for lifting and moving vessels. Looking at
the miniature steamship, about seven feet in length, standing
on the railway of the model, he said to Mr. Eads, with intense
earnestness : "I actually see that steamship moving through
"the tropical forests of Tehuantepec, on its journey from
"ocean to ocean. I now am firmly convinced of its prac-
"ticability, and will double my subscription."

Closing an elaborate and accurate description of this
model, the *London Times* of August 1st, 1884, says :

"Looking at the Ship Railway project from a broad and
"general point of view, there can be little doubt that it is
"one which is fraught with great results. This will be
"better realized when it is remembered that the American
"Isthmus separates about 100,000,000 of the most enter-
"prising, industrious amd enlightened people on the face of
"the earth, inhabiting the North Atlantic coasts of Europe
"and America, from 600,000,000 who inhabit the Orient and
"the Islands of the Pacific. It is true that the sailing
"distances which separate England from India, China and
"other Oriental countries, have been greatly reduced by the
"Suez Canal ; but these distances are almost insignificant
"when compared with those which the Ship Railway would
"annihilate. For instance, the great saving effected by the
"Suez Canal between London and Calcutta, is about 4,500
"statute miles, whereas the sailing distance by the Ship
"Railway from London to every port on the Pacific coast of
"North America, will be lessened by nearly twice this great
"distance or about 8,250 miles. The Suez Canal brought
"London and Canton about 3,500 miles nearer together by
"sea. The Ship Railway would save more than three times
"that distance between the great American metropolis and

" every port in British Columbia. The American Isthmus
" and the Cordilleras of North America constitute a narrow
" but almost impassable barrier to the interchange of the
" manufactures and productions of 40,000,000 of people in
" the Mississippi Valley and Atlantic States, not only
" with those of 10,000,000 of their countrymen to the west of
" them, but with others on the islands and coasts of the
" Pacific who are seemingly their nearest neighbors. The
" Ship Railway would give to these descendants of the
" British Isles, a sea route between their Atlantic and Pacific
" ports scarcely a thousand miles longer than the railway
" between New York and San Francisco, and it would give
" to the vast Valley of the Mississippi, a gateway equivalent
" to the discharge of its mighty river directly into the
" Pacific."

## SECOND.

### PRACTICABILITY.

It has been truly said, that all new ideas and enterprises
must pass through three stages before reaching complete
recognition, or realization, viz :—ridicule, possibility and
probability. This has been the history of all newly discovered truths and of all new ideas carried into actual practice.
This is notably seen in the successful realization of agricultural, astronomical, dynamic and electric principles and ideas.
The world is round and revolves; the stars in the vault of
heaven are other worlds ; the force of steam drives the
locomotive and gives it power and speed; the electric wires
are spun through the valleys and over the mountains, flashing
thoughts from mind to mind, and under the waters of the sea
the Atlantic cables interchange in a moment the thoughts of
the continents ; and yet each one of these ideas was once
scouted as untrue or impracticable and its teachers and ad-
vocates were looked upon as the veriest visionaries.

The proposition of Mr. James B. Eads, to transport large
vessels overland across the American Isthmus, has, in the
minds of thinking men and of experts whose attention has
been given to it, passed through the two preliminary stages—

ridicule and possibility—and is now in the stage of probability. Nothing is required to advance it to the stage of certainty and of complete realization but the necessary means for doing the mechanical work and constructing a roadway for the ingeniously designed carriage for transporting vessels.

The obstacles to be overcome by mechanical ingenuity were, first, the distribution of weight so that the parts of the carriage, and particularly the wheels, should not be unduly loaded, and second, the adaptation of the carriage to the ship, so as not, in any possible manner, to injure the hull or strain any part of it beyond what it was designed to bear on the ocean. Principles and appliances long known and employed in lifting and moving vessels are used, with some special adaptations only, to enable them to be transported with greater speed than they are usually moved on inclined railways.

The history of vessel moving and transporting overland is ancient. The Athenians, centuries before the christian era, transported their war ships, of probably one hundred and fifty tons, across the Isthmus of Corinth, about fourteen miles. Loaded canal boats and other vessels of considerable tonnage have been hauled on carriages overland on railways and over long distances up and down steep gradients.

In the lifting of vessels from the water to a higher level, three methods were found practicable and in use in various parts of the world. First by an inclined railway, second by a positive hydraulic lift with presses or rams, and third by a floating pontoon or caisson  Although the original plans contemplated the use of the inclined railway, the idea was abandoned for several reasons, especially as it would require a railway extending under water a long distance into the sea, where it would be difficult to maintain the track intact; it would also be much more expensive than other methods. Responsible parties were found who lifted loaded vessels, up to twelve thousand tons weight, by a vertical hydraulic lift, and who agreed to construct a dock of this kind that would lift a vessel weighing ten thousand tons, on a carriage suitable for transportation over land, to a height of forty-six feet and place the vessel and carriage upon the railway, all in thirty minutes time. They proposed also to build locomotives that would haul these loads over ordinary grades. However, after mature consideration of the detailed plans and estimates of cost, it was decided to lift the vessels by pontoons or floating docks, the ordinary method in use in all commercial countries. The comparatively rude methods of docking and adjusting loaded vessels on a floating dock require modification, as it is necessary not only to lift the vessel on the pontoon, but to place her on a carriage with her weight so equalized from stem to stern as to enable the carriage to move easily and safely. This distribution of weight and transfer of the distributed weight to the carriage is effected as follows:—The pontoon is capable of raising easily a vessel of five thousand tons gross weight, this being as large as the Isthmian business will employ, for the present at least. The size of the pontoon is about 450 feet long, 75 feet wide and 15 feet deep, arranged with a system of hydraulic rams placed on an intermediate deck about six feet below the upper deck of the pontoon. These rams are arranged in lateral and longitudinal lines, the former being placed a little less than seven feet apart. The area of the combined rams in each lateral line is the same—for example, the area of the one ram under the keel at the bow or stern is equal to the area of the five or seven rams amidships. These rams are, or can be, all connected together, so that the same pressure per square inch of surface of the rams, exists throughout the whole system, or they can be disconnected by valves so that a greater pressure can be brought upon the rams in a certain section or on a certain line. These rams are not intended to lift the vessel, but simply to resist its weight when it comes up out of the water. They are actuated by a powerful hydraulic pump, erected on a tower attached to the side of the pontoon and rising and sinking with it, but of sufficient height above it to not become submerged when the pontoon is grounded on the bottom of the basin or dock. The pontoon is guided in its upward or downward movement by strong anchor rods, or columns, passing through it freely, and firmly secured in the foundations of the dock.

The carriage for supporting and moving the vessel will be

arranged to move on six rails—three standard gauge tracks each of 4 feet 8½ inches. As the ship is itself a girder, fore and aft, and will not be bent in that direction on an immovable roadway, the maximum strength of the carriage is in the cross girders which are spaced like the lateral lines of the rams, about seven feet apart, and are of sufficient depth and have sufficient material in their plates to transfer equal loads to all the wheels. The wheels are double flanged, placed as near together as is necessary to distribute the weight and are each hung independently to its own journals, with an independent axle for each wheel. The system of trucks, of four or six wheels, movable about a central pin, on which cars are supported on an ordinary railroad, is not required in the ship railway carriage, as it is intended to move the loads on straight lines, curves not being admissible in a rigid carriage of such great length. Over each wheel is a powerful spring which will bear twenty or more tons before closing. It has a vertical movement of about six inches. The maximum load on a level track will not close these springs more than three inches, thus permitting the carriage to pass over any irregularities which might occur, without bringing any undue weight upon the wheels. They also furnish a complete elastic bearing for the loaded vessel, and will permit it to move on the carriage easily over the railway without any possibility of jar or strain. Upon the model is arranged a system of supports for the vessel with adjustable surfaces hinged to the top of the supports by a toggle joint, so as to fit the shape of the hull at every point. The supports on the outside line are fitted with adjustable hinged girths covered with a rubber or other cushioned surface. These supports, or rods, or columns, pass through the girders of the carriage freely and are exactly pendant over the hydraulic rams when the carriage is on the pontoon, locked in proper and exact position. The carriage having been run on the pontoon, when it is floating, and the surface of its rails exactly corresponding with the rails of the permanent way on shore, the water is let into the compartments of the pontoon and it, with the carriage, is sunk to the bottom and grounded on the cross bearers of the dock. The ship is then brought from the exterior basin into the dock over the carriage, and so adjusted that her keel is exactly over the continuous keel block of the carriage, and her centre of gravity, as near as possible, over the central point in the length of the carriage. The water is then pumped out of the pontoon by a powerful centrifugal pump and it rises towards the hull of the vessel. When the keel block of the carriage is about two feet from the keel of the vessel, the hydraulic pump is started, pushing up the pendant rods and posts of the supports gently against the vessel, under the keel, bottom and bilges, and snugly up around the sides. As the vessel continues to rise and her weight increases, the pressure upon the rams increases, but the water pressure under them being prevented from escaping by closing the valves, the full weight of the vessel, when she is entirely out of the water, is borne on the rams ; they having conformed their movement to the shape of the vessel.

Assuming, for illustration, that there are fifty lines of rams and that the ship weighs five thousand tons, then each line of rams will have imposed upon it a weight of one hundred tons, no more and no less. As these lines of rams are spaced equally from stem to stern, and each upholds a weight of one hundred tons, then the weight of the ship must be borne equally each unit of its length. The pressure gauge on the hydraulic pump will indicate the exact weight or displacement of the vessel, and may form the basis for ascertaining the charge for transporting her. When the ship is entirely out of the water, hand wheels, or adjusting nuts, moving in threads cut in the columns of the supports, are run down by the workmen to a bearing on the girder plates ; the rams are then withdrawn by opening the valve and the girders support the evenly distributed weight of the vessel. As an equal number of wheels are placed with each girder, and each girder, by the arrangement just mentioned, upholds its exact proportion of the load, then all the wheels, from one end to the other of the carriage, must have equal weights imposed upon them—that is, not over eight or nine tons, which is an admissible load, since much larger weights are carried upon the wheels of ordinary locomotives and other rolling stock, both in the United States and Europe. Each wheel will be tested to twenty tons.

The adjustable supports of the carriage can be made to fit neatly and bear evenly upon any vessel that ranges in beam between certain limits, and for smaller or larger vessels than these limits, different sizes of carriages will be constructed, with a modification of the lines of the supports.

It will not always be possible to place a vessel, when brought into the dock, immediately over the exact centre of the pontoon ; the result will be that when the weight of the vessel is brought on the pontoon, one end will have a tendency to sink and the other to rise. This is overcome, and the pontoon balanced by hydrostatic pressure in what are called "hydraulic governors," as follows :—Two cylinders are attached to each corner of the dock, one being upright and the other inverted. Plungers, attached to the pontoon, move in them. The cylinders on diagonal corners are connected by pipes, and all spaces in the cylinders and pipes are filled solid with water. As the pontoon rises, the water forced out of one cylinder by the ascending plunger is forced into the inverted cylinder on the diagonal corner where the plunger is being withdrawn. Now, if there is, say one hundred tons preponderance on one end of the pontoon, one half this weight, or fifty tons pressure, will be exerted by each plunger on that end upon the water in its cylinder. This pressure is instantaneously transmitted through the pipes to the water in the top of the upright cylinder on the diagonal corner, which acts with the same amount of pressure, as a water plunger, upon the metal plunger to hold it down ; thus an equilibrium is maintained and the pontoon compelled to rise and fall perfectly level.

It is possible by the aid of a pressure gauge attached to the pipes to ascertain the exact amount of the excess of weight, so that should this gauge show too great a preponderance, the pontoon must be lowered and the ship placed in a new position. When the pontoon has risen so that the surfaces of the rails laid upon it are exactly level with those of the railway, it is prevented from rising further by the heads of the anchor bolts, or guiding rods, which are also sufficiently strong to prevent one end of the pontoon rising, when the carriage, with the vessel upon it is being run off. In practice these anchor rods will be large hollow cylindrical columns filled with heavy material to give them weight.

The railway will be built on practically straight lines, a curve of less than twenty miles radius not being admissible, with a rigid carriage four hundred feet in length. There are, however, five points on the isthmus, as located by the surveys, where it will be necessary to make quite abrupt changes in direction in order to avoid heavy construction work. The railway in this section of the country, on the table lands, follows a succession of broad valleys flanked by ranges of hills or spurs of the Sierra Madre, and to pass from one valley to another, or from one plain to another, it is necessary to make deflections where there is not sufficient open country to use curves of the radius named. At these five points, the changes in direction are made by floating turntables, which are no more nor less than floating pontoons large enough to take the carriage with the ship and float it about a central pivot, or cylinder. The pontoon, when the carriage with the vessel is run upon it, is solidly grounded, by the weight of water in it, upon the circular bearers in the basin. The carriage is placed on the centre of the pontoon and the water is pumped out by means of a powerful centrifugal pump, withdrawing the water through an opening in the cylindrical pivot of the pontoon and discharging it into the basin. When sufficient flotation has been given to the pontoon by this means to slightly raise it from its bearing surfaces, it is moved about the pivot by steam power in the direction required ; the water is then admitted to it through valves, and it is grounded again upon the bearers in the basin. The locomotives then move the vessel in the new direction. These turntables, or pontoons, by laying several radial tracks, can be utilized for passing points and also for standing vessels, for painting, or repairs, if desired. The simplicity and economy of this method of turning vessels is particularly noted by those who have seen the working model illustrating it. No adjustments are required, and the level of the pontoon, when floating, can be very easily secured by admitting water into one or more compartments at either end of it. As the weight of the vessel is equalized over the whole length of the carriage the central point of the carriage cannot be far from the centre of gravity of the load.

The motive power for hauling the vessels over the railway will not be difficult to design or build ; it is simply a question of amount of power. We know that loads up to two thousand tons are now hauled on ordinary railways by the freight engines of the day. If one of these engines will haul a train of half a mile in length over the grades and around the curves of our railways at a rate of speed of from fifteen to twenty miles per hour, will any one question the ability of locomotives especially designed and of great traction power, to move easily a compact mass on three straight tracks with the opportunity of attaching, if necessary, three engines in front and three in the rear of the carriage ?

In reference to the above description it should be stated, that the working plans of full-sized works—pontoon, carriage and floating turntable, have been reduced in scale to the size of a working model which, when the parts are connected, is about thirty feet in length, with a perfect modeled steamer about 7½ feet long. This working model will, if thoroughly examined and its principles understood, dissipate any prejudice that exists against the practicability of the ship railway, and convince any fair minded person that it is perfectly practicable to lift and transfer vessels with their cargoes on board, in such a manner as, in no wise, to injure any seaworthy vessel, or the integrity of the carriage upon which it is transported. Over one thousand scientific and practical men in London saw this model ; they were the representatives of the civil and mechanical engineers, ship builders, ship owners, dock builders, capitalists and commercial men. The universally expressed opinion was cordially in favor of the entire practicability of the Ship Railway. In the city of New York at this writing, over seven thousand people have witnessed the movements and action of this model ; many were from the same classes as in London, and their expressed verdict has been the same. However, as this model can be seen by only a few persons, the objections which may be brought forward by those not perfectly familiar with the methods proposed, will be briefly stated and answered.

First objection : Injury to the vessel by the outward pressure of the cargo when she is taken out of the water.

Answer : When the vessel is in, what is called, its " natural " element, she undergoes, often, unnatural and more severe strains than in docking. The sudden withdrawal of the water pressure when the vessel in a heavy sea rides, bow and stern, on two huge waves, would cause her sides to burst out if she were not specially constructed to withstand just such pressure. A heavy sea, rolling its great waves one after another alongside the vessel from bow to stern, with the hollow of the waves following quickly, would seem to be productive, if any possible condition could be, of the opening of the vessel's sides. The fact is, the bursting pressure is less than is imagined. Every elevator or grain cargo box is more likely to be pressed outwards or downwards by its load of grain, than is a vessel's sides when out of the water.

Second objection :  Injury to the bottom of the vessel by supporting it by artificial means when the cargo is on board.

Answer :  It should be clearly understood that the hydraulic press system, which first holds up the vessel when she is out of the water is, as it were, so many columns of water under the vessel, gently and effectually equalizing her weight. If in the process of raising, the support raised by one ram comes in contact with the keel, bottom, bilges or sides of the vessel, it will exert no pressure until all the other rams have reached a point of contact, and then the pressure per square inch of ram surface is the same throughout the whole system. The rams of the greatest area are placed under the keel where the load is the greatest and the vessel most able to withstand heavy pressure. Over the whole surface of the hull, wherever it has any bearing upon the water, the full, complete and adjustable system of supports is spread, with their broad and cushioned surfaces. Vessels of the most ancient and decayed skin and timbers, if seaworthy, can be carried on this perfectly equalized system of supports, and be in effect water-borne. In reference to both these objections, Mr. E. A. Fuertes, Professor in the Department of Civil

Engineering of Cornell University, N. Y., gives very valuable testimony in reference to some examinations he made on the White Star line steamer "Germanic," on the voyage between Liverpool and New York. These examinations, made while the vessel was moving through an ordinary sea, were for the purpose of ascertaining the concave and convex flexures of the steamer in the direction of her length. He found that the total deflection in a distance of 264 feet was 13 inches, or $6\frac{1}{2}$ inches above and below the mean line. Comparing the effects of a heavy sea upon an iron steamer with the effects upon the same steamer, when carried upon a properly designed and constructed railway, he speaks of the strain upon the vessel when a sinking or receding sea instantly withdraws the volumes of water pressure from against her sides, and the reaction of her frame when, with equal suddenness, it feels the pressure of her cargo, if any such pressure exists.

" Also the sea strikes blows with concentrated vigor upon
" the restricted area of the ship's surface, causing the dreaded
" tremor from stem to stern, and working her joints and tim-
" bers with all kinds of flexures, tortions and impacts. Only
" those who have had personal experience with the sea in a
" hurricane can realize the stiffness required in a sea-going
" vessel.

" It is strange to see how strongly intolerant popular mis-
" conceptions can be in questions of this kind. While a ship
" must be constructed so that it may stand safely on end or
" be shaken violently when held in the middle or by her ex-
" tremities, the popular prejudice against a ship railway is
" based upon the assumption that all ships are wanting in
" the very quality that they must possess, viz : stiffness."

The following statement of opinions and facts upon this subject will support the views advanced above. A letter, dated February 14th, 1882, from Mr. William S. Buckley, President of the New York Balance Dock Company, gives a list of five ships and six steamers, ranging from about 2,000 to 2,700 tons, that were taken out on his dock with cargoes in them. In this letter Mr. Buckley says : " We do not refuse
" any class of ships or steamers, even with coals and cargoes

"on board, whose length does not exceed the length of the
" dock. In every case in which we have taken up steamers
" with the cargoes in, it has been done without the least
" strain 'or injury to the vessel. As the rule is to make a
" charge for raising the cargo on a vessel, they usually come
" to us without cargo."

Mr. Edward Hart, U. S. Naval Constructor, in a letter to
Mr. Eads, says (quoting a portion, only, appertaining to this
subject) :

" With a substantial road-bed for your Ship Railway, on the
" easy grades across Tehuantepec, which I understand do
" not exeed .one or two feet in the hundred, there can be no
" mechanical difficulty in the way of transporting loaded ships
" by railroad with entire safety to the vessels, whether they
" be built of wood or iron." Mr. Hart is one of the oldest and
ablest constructors in the U. S. Navy.

Mr. H. L. Fernald, a Constructor of the U. S. Navy of re-
cognized ability and talent, stated in a letter as follows':

" Having carefully examined the plans and papers per-
" taining to the proposed Ship Railway across the Isthmus of
" Tehuantepec, I do not hesitate to say that in my judgment
" there will be no difficulty whatever in transporting in the
" manner you propose any properly built vessel with absolute
" safety."

The London *Iron*, of October 3d, 1884, in brief but com-
prehensive language, sets at rest any fears that may exist in
the minds of timorous people in reference to the injury that
vessels may sustain by being docked and handled with the
cargo on board :

" The question of endangering the structural integrity of a ship
" loaded with cargo by taking her out of the water and placing her
" on intermediate supports, is one which has frequently been raised
" only to be summarily disposed of by those who give the matter a
" moment's thought. As, however, there is still a popular notion
" that a loaded vessel under such conditions is subject to injurious
" strains, it may be as well if we point out how utterly impossible
" this is by reason of the construction of the vessel itself. No greater
' fallacy than this was ever conceived, for there is no form of struc-

, " ture which is known to be subject to more unequal, irregular and
" ever-varying strains than a ship at sea, and these very points are
" carefully provided against in her design and construction. A prop-
" erly designed and constructed ship resembles a girder, and is so
" built that no matter how she may be tossed about on the waves,
" the strains, conflicting and almost puzzling as they are, are dis-
" tributed equally through her framing and plating or planking. If
" there was any fear of her cargo bursting her sides, as some have
" held there is, it would have burst them on her first loading, as, al-
" though water is incompressible in confinement, it is exceedingly ·
" yielding when unconfined. Hence the risk of damage to vessels
" by straining during transport overland, may at once be set aside as
" puerile, especially in the face of the ingenious arrangement de-
" signed by Mr. Eads for equalising their support. Moreover, the
" raising of ships with their cargoes, from a lower to a higher level,
" by means of hydraulic lifts, has been successfully accomplished for
" long past. The Victoria Docks, in London, and those at Malta
" and Bombay, have been operated for years without an accident.
" Again, it is a matter of common occurrence to keep loaded vessels
" for days, and even weeks, upon dry docks for repairs, and then re-
" turn them to water without the slightest strain or injury."

The most valuable expert testimony that has been given on
this subject, is by Sir Edward Reed, K. C. B., late Chief Constructor of the British Navy. The testimony was given before the Committee on Commerce of the United States Senate. The following quotations are from his testimony, and
bear directly on this special subject :

" I have no hesitancy in saying that the marine ships of to-
" day are vastly stronger everywhere than they were half a
" century ago, and that they are now, as a rule, perfectly ca-
" pable of being docked in dry docks with their cargoes on
" board.

" I would like to say first, that there is no fear whatever
" of a ship undergoing any strain in the process of lifting out
" of the water (as would be necessary in case of a ship rail-
" way) that she is not liable to at present in ordinary dock-
" ing.

" I would say further, that I am quite sure that the pro-
" cesses of ordinary docking, as carried on in a vast number

" of private establishments, are very negligent and insuffi-
" cient in comparison with those which would be adopted in
" case of the hydraulic lifts connected with the proposed ship
" railway."

In reference to the hydraulic docks at Malta he gives a
list of several vessels docked with their cargoes on board, and
states : "I would call attention to the fact that although
"ship owners were at first afraid of docking ships in that way
"with their cargoes on board, they have discovered by the
"experience of years that no sort of injury does result,
" for all the ships that are in the Indian trade now voluntarily
" employ these docks and go upon them with their cargoes
"on board for the purpose of getting their bottoms cleaned
"and coated on the voyage, instead of having to lie in a more
" expensive dock in London, for the purpose."

Mr. William Pierce, sole proprietor of the John Elder &
Company's works, Govan, Glasgow, and who built the "Ari-
zona," the " Elbe," and the "Alaska," and others of the finest
steamers afloat, says in a letter : " I am of the opinion from
" what I know of the working of iron floating docks that I
" have designed and built, that iron steamers of 4,000 to
" 5,000 tons displacement, may be docked loaded with-
" out any injury whatever."

Commander T. D. Wilson, Chief Constructor of the U. S.
Navy, states as follows : "I see no good reason why any
" vessel cannot be successfully raised and transported upon a
" properly constructed railway, with a grade as stated, if
" reasonable skill and care are used in the work, and I believe
" the strain she will be subjected to will be inferior to those.
" which ocean steamers are constantly exposed to."

Objections of various kinds have been raised to the plan of
lifting vessels out of the water, and transporting them, but it
is useless to enter into any further argument in regard to it
in the face of the numerous and well authenticated facts
which go to show that vessels are, in all parts of the world,
very frequently docked with their cargoes on board without
the least injury to the vessel. The only injury that can possibly happen to them under these circumstances, is by care-

less handling or by not taking precautions against the strains that might possibly be engendered in lifting the vessel. If it is once admitted that the vessel can be docked with the cargo on board, it must also be admitted that ships can be hauled on a properly designed and constructed railway carriage without injury.

As the practicability of the Ship Railway depends in a measure upon the character of the country where it is to be constructed and operated, that country will be briefly described from facts gathered by careful surveys and detailed examinations made during five months by the writer himself, and during seventeen months by an able and skillful corps of civil engineers.

The Isthmus of Tehuantepec lies immediately north (or west) of the promontory of Yucatan. It is the narrowest part of the Isthmus in Mexico. A line drawn from the terminus of the Ship Railway on the Gulf to the terminus on the Pacific, is almost due north and south. The terminus on the north is on the banks of the Coatzacoalcos River at the town of Minatitlan, situated about twenty-five miles from the mouth of the river. This is a broad deep river and requires improvement by artificial means at only one point. This can be done easily and inexpensively by judiciously constructed dykes or wing dams. At the mouth of the river is a bar, formed by the river's deposit, and which it is designed to deepen by jetties similar to those at the mouth of the Mississippi River. There is now about fifteen feet depth of water over the bar. The line of the railway from Minatitlan follows the gently ascending Atlantic plains over firm, unyielding ground. At about thirty-five miles from Minatitlan the railway will be constructed through a gently undulating table land, and then will follow a series of broad valleys reaching the Tarifa plains, which is the summit level, 726 feet above the level of the sea. The descent from that point to the Pacific plains requires three deflecting turntables to avoid heavy excavations and give the necessary distance required to preserve an uniformly descending grade of one per cent. From the base of the mountains to the Pacific terminus the line extends over a nearly level country. The terminal on the Pacific side is a matter of choice simply, two good locations having been found—one at Salina Cruz, and the other on one of the Lagoons or Lakes. The climate is salubrious and healthy. It needs only to be said in support of this statement that a corps of several unacclimated young men, from the northern portions of the United States went to the Isthmus just before the rainy season commenced, remained there through it, and were not off duty through any sickness while engaged upon the work. Some of them remained seventeen months. Mr. Deming J. Thayer, engineeer in charge, recently returned from the Isthmus, states in his report :

" Hitherto it has been erroneously supposed that engineer-" ing parties could not remain in the field during the rainy " season ; that the increase in hardships would result in sick-" ness among the men employed, and this, in connection ": with the time lost when rainy, would render desirable pro-" gress impossible. Our experience during an entire and un-" usually hard rainy season, disproves this supposition. No " sickness showed itself among the assistants or men ; little " or no time was lost, and progress was nearly as rapid as " during the dry season."

The character of the laborers to be obtained on the Isthmus, from the people residing there, is exceptionally good, especially on the Pacific slope, which is inhabited by a hardy and industrious race of agricultural people. From eight thousand to ten thousand laborers can be obtained from among them. The very best materials for the construction of the Ship Railway can be found on the Isthmus in convenient locations. Many varieties of timber, very durable in character and suitable for either temporary or permanent work in construction, are found throughout nearly the entire line. Good building stone, granite, limestone, sandstone, and other varieties are at hand. available for purposes of construction. The direction of such winds as are prevalent coincides very nearly with the line of the railway. The very frail construction of the principal portion of the houses on the Isthmus, covered as they are with large and high palm roofs, extending beyond, and generally separate from their walls ; the exposed places in which many of them stand,

and the absence of any evidence of injury to them, is proof that very strong winds are unknown on the Isthmus. The whole country along and near the proposed line has been covered by accurate instrumental surveys under the direction of experienced engineers. The elaborate and extensive surveys of Mr. Martin Van Brocklin, Resident Engineer, have not only demonstrated the entire practicability of the construction of a railway sufficiently solid to carry any load that could possibly be imposed upon it in the transportation of the largest vessels, but have also made it possible to locate the line for construction. They have also been sufficiently detailed to admit a reliable estimate to be made of the cost ; and they have furnished all possible information needed as to materials for construction, obstacles to be met, and the means of overcoming them.

We are convinced, therefore, that it is practicable beyond any doubt to construct the mechanical appliances for lifting and transporting vessels and to build a railway sufficiently solid and permanent to carry the loads at any desired speed ; all without injury to the vessels or the carriages that transport them.

Among a large number of experts, practical and experienced men, who have examined the physical and mechanical conditions and obstacles, and pronounced the work practicable, we will, in conclusion, mention but a few of those whose decided opinions had much weight with the Committee of the U. S. Senate, and which, confirming the results of its own examination, led it to report unanimously in favor of the practicability of the Ship Railway. Sir Edward J. Reed, late Chief Constructor of the British Navy (already alluded to) gave most forcible and convincing testimony before this committee as to the practicability of the Ship Railway, and fortified his opinion by statements of facts impossible to refute. Mr. Nathaniel Barnaby, present Chief Constructor of the British Navy, stated that the problem of carrying loaded ships on a railway was not only soluble, but that the solution was fairly indicated in the plans shown him by Mr. Eads. Mr. William John, for some years the scientific adviser of the committee of Lloyd's Register, stated that the lifting of vessels out of the water having become an every day occurrence, the work of placing them on a carriage and transporting them was a simple matter.

Mr. John Fowler, a civil engineer of Great Britain, of wide reputation, has himself proposed and designed plans for transporting vessels overland from one level to another at the first cataract of the Nile. Mr. George Fosbury Lyster, Engineer in Chief of the Liverpool docks, closes a decided opinion on the subject by saying : " There will, in my judgment, be little or " no difficulty in transporting properly constructed ships " from sea to sea with entire convenience and safety." The firm of Emerson, Murgotroyd & Co., who constructed the great hydraulic docks at Malta and Bombay, agreed with Mr. Eads that they would lift for the Tehuantepec Ship Railway loaded ships of from 8,000 to 10,000 tons weight on a railway car and place them on the permanent way in thirty minutes ; agreeing also to build the car and locomotives and ten miles of the railway, and to guarantee the safe transportation of the loaded ships over the railway.

Messrs. Leader Williams and B. Baker, both prominent civil engineers of England ; Prof. Elgar, General Manager of Earls Ship Building and Engineering Co., and Mr. Martell of Lloyds, have added important testimony to the entire practicability of the Ship Railway. In the United States, strong supporting opinions from able men have not been wanting. Genenal Q. A. Gillmore, a distinguished engineer of the United States, says in a letter :

"In my judgment the construction of a ship railway across " the Mexican Isthmus, in general accordance with your plan, " is not only feasible as an engineering problem, but the suc- " cessful maintenance and operation of such a road is entirely " practicable as a business enterprise."

Major Charles R. Suter, another able engineer of the United States Army, says : " The project has great and ob- " vious advantages to recommend it and, from an engineering " point of view, it is, in my opinion, perfectly practicable."

General G. T. Beauregard, Colonel Henry Flad, Mr. O. Chanute, Mr. T. C. Clarke, Mr. J. J. Williams and other civil engineers of high reputation in the United States, have given favorable and decided views on the subject.

After canvassing this whole subject of the practicability of the Ship Railway, the Senate Committee summed up the evidence as follows :

"The testimony upon the subject, is so overwhelming and " conclusive in its character, that the committee has no hesi- " tation in reporting that the construction of a ship railway, " and its successful operation, are *entirely practicable.*"

## THIRD.

### ADVANTAGES.

The construction and operation of a Ship Railway at Tehuantepec having been shown to be practicable, it is only necessary to give the imagination wings to see the poetic prophecy of the poet Wordsworth transformed into reality, when in the " Highland Broach " he says :

> "Lo ! ships, from seas by nature barred,
> Mount along ways by man prepared."

We may safely utter the prophecy, not poetical, but practical, that the tall masts of ocean steamers will, as in a panorama, pass among the palms of the plains of Tarifa, in their journey from ocean to ocean.

For many years, not only have the leading statesmen of Mexico appreciated the advantages of the Tehuantepec route for an inter-oceanic crossing, but the statesmen of the United States have been impressed with the importance of these advantages.

Daniel Webster, while Secretary of State, in 1851, said in an official letter :  " No one can fail to see how exceedingly " important this communication would be to the Government " of Mexico.  It proposes to give her a practical highway " from sea to sea.  It opens to her a communication on the " one side and on the other with the eastern and western " world.  It gives her access to the markets of all nations, and " makes her, in short, the central point of the commerce of " modern times."

Said that illustrious statesman, Lewis Cass, in an official letter while Secretary of State, in 1857 : " The proximity of " the isthmus to our shores, the salubrity of the climate, " the adaptness of the ground for the construction of the " railroad, and the great diminution of distance in comparison " with traveled routes between our Atlantic and Pacific pos- " sessions, all conspire to point it out as far preferable to any " other route."

Commodore Shufeldt, in 1871, in an official report of his survey of the Isthmus of Tehuantepec, said : " Each isthmus " rises into importance as it lies nearer to the centre of Amer- " ican commercial interests ; and the intrinsic value of this " eminently national work ought to be based upon the inverse " ratio of the distance from that centre."

An inter-oceanic crossing, according to his report, would be an extension of the Mississippi River to the Pacific Ocean, which would convert the Gulf into an American lake, and, so to speak, render our own territory circumnavigable ; and the character of the intervening water is such, that it would permit a canal boat to load at St. Louis and discharge her freight in California with but little more than the risk of inland navigation.

That great geographer, known the world over for the results of his patient, long-continued studies of ocean currents, Lieut. Maury, whose eloquence is only exceeded by the correctness and breadth of his opinions, once said of this American inland sea, from which it is proposed to transport vessels to the Pacific : " From the Gulf of Mexico, the great commercial mar- " kets of the world are down-hill. A vessel bound from that " gulf to Europe places herself in the current of the Gulf Stream " and drifts along with it at the rate, for part of the way, of " eighty or one hundred miles a day. * * * And " when there shall be established a commercial thoroughfare " across the isthmus, the trade winds of the Pacific will place " China, India, New Holland and all the islands of that ocean " down-hill from this sea of ours. In that case, Europe must " pass by our very doors on the great highway to the markets " both of the East and West Indies. This beautiful Mesopo-

" tamian sea is in a position to occupy the summit level of
" navigation and to become the great commercial receptacle
" of the world. Our rivers run into it, and float down with
" their currents the surplus articles of merchandise that are
" produced upon their banks. Arrived with them upon the
" bosom of this grand marine basin, there are the currents of
" the sea and the winds of heaven, so arranged by nature that
" they drift it and waft it down-hill and down stream to the
" great market-places of the world. * * * The area of
" all the valleys which are drained by the rivers of Europe
" that empty into the Atlantic ; of all the valleys that are
" drained by the rivers of Asia, which empty into the In-
" dian Ocean, and of all the valleys that are drained by the
" rivers of Africa and Europe which empty into the Med-
" iterranean, does not cover an extent of territory as great as
" that included in the valleys drained by the American rivers
" alone which discharge themselves into our central sea.
" Never was there such a concentration upon any sea, of com-
" mercial resources ; never was there a sea known with such
" a back country tributary to it,"

The advantages to be gained are so great, the benefits to
commerce and the world are so important, that they will
sooner or later impress themselves so deeply in the minds of
this impatient generation, that nothing but a realized inter-
oceanic communication for ships will in any way satisfy it.
When we contemplate the changes that will certainly take
place in, not only commerce, but agriculture and manufactures, and further still, in the general development of the
nations by the immense reduction in the distances that now
lie between them, the most sanguine cannot comprehend these
grand and forever increasing benefits. The map of the world
shows the Isthmus of Tehuantepec to lie midway in almost
direct lines from the whole eastern coasts of Australia and
Asia, to all our Gulf and Atlantic ports and the ports of Western Europe. The following tables of comparative distances
show the great saving in time by the Tehuantepec route :

# TABLE OF COMPARATIVE DISTANCES IN STATUTE MILES.

| | Total Distance. | Excess over Tehuantepec Route. |
|---|---|---|
| **FROM NEW YORK TO HONG KONG.** | | |
| Via Cape Horn.............................. | 20,370 miles. | 8,777 miles. |
| Cape of Good Hope................. ....... | 16,045 | 5,343 |
| Suez Canal ... ............... .......... ... | 13,596 | 1,994 |
| Panama R. R....... ...................... | 12,953 | 1,351 |
| Isthmus of Tehuantepec.................. | 11,602 | .... |
| **NEW YORK TO YOKOHAMA.** | | |
| Via Cape Horn.............................. | 19,802 | 9,796 |
| Cape of Good Hope..................... | 18,085 | 8,079 |
| Suez Canal.... ..................... | 15,527 | 5,521 |
| Panama R. R.............................. | 11,256 | 1,250 |
| Isthmus of Tehuantepec.................. | 10,006 | .... |
| **NEW YORK TO AUCKLAND, N. Z.** | | |
| Via Suez Canal.............................. | 16,871 | 7,447 |
| Cape of Good Hope...................... | 16,719 | 7,295 |
| Cape Horn.............................. | 13,890 | 4,466 |
| Panama R. R.............................. | 10,305 | 881 |
| Isthmus of Tehuantepec.................. | 9,424 | .... |
| **NEW YORK TO MELBOURNE.** | | |
| Via Cape Horn.............................. | 15,215 | 4,150 |
| Suez Canal.............................. | 15,171 | 4,106 |
| Cape of Good Hope...................... | 15,019 | 3,954 |
| Panama R. R.............................. | 11,826 | 761 |
| Isthmus of Tehuantepec ............... | 11,065 | .... |
| **NEW YORK TO HONOLULU.** | | |
| Via Cape Horn............. ................. | 15,826 | 9,163 |
| Panama R. R.............................. | 7,939 | 1,276 |
| Isthmus of Tehuantepec............... . | 6,663 | .... |
| **NEW YORK TO SAN FRANCISCO.** | | |
| Via Cape Horn..... ....................... | 15,687 | 10,797 |
| Panama R. R.............................. | 6,063 | 1,173 |
| Isthmus of Tehuantepec.................. | 4,890 | .... |
| **LIVERPOOL TO HONG KONG.** | | |
| Via Cape Horn.............................. | 20,606 | 5,353 |
| Panama R. R................. .......... | 16,471 | 1,218 |
| Cape of Good Hope...................... | 15,722 | 469 |
| Isthmus of Tehuantepec... ............. | 15,253 | .... |
| **LIVERPOOL TO YOKOHAMA.** | | |
| Via Cape Horn.............................. | 19,400 | 5,945 |
| Cape of Good Hope.................... | 17,653 | 4,198 |
| Panama R. R.............................. | 14,540 | 1,085 |
| Isthmus of Tehuantepec........ .......... | 13,455 | .... |
| **LIVERPOOL TO AUCKLAND, N. Z.** | | |
| Via Cape of Good Hope................ ....... | 16,221 | 3,412 |
| Suez Canal.... .. ..................... | 14,645 | 1,836 |
| Cape Horn.............................. | 13,897 | 1,088 |
| Panama R. R.... ..... ...... ......... | 13,312 | 503 |
| Isthmus of Tehuantepec...... ........... | 12,809 | .... |

# TABLE OF COMPARATIVE DISTANCES IN STATUTE MILES.

| | Total Distance. | Excess over Tehuantepec Route. |
|---|---|---|
| **LIVERPOOL TO SAN FRANCISCO.** | | |
| Via Cape Horn......................... .... | 15,803 | 7,527 |
| Panama R. R............................ | 8,885 | 609 |
| Isthmus of Tehuantepec................. | 8,276 | .... |
| **NEW ORLEANS TO HONG KONG** | | |
| Via Cape Horn.............................. | 20,804 | 10,531 |
| Cape of Good Hope........................ | 17,485 | 7,212 |
| Suez Canal .............................. | 15,108 | 4,835 |
| Panama R. R.............................. | 12,308 | 2,035 |
| Isthmus of Tehuantepec................. | 10,273 | .... |
| **NEW ORLEANS TO YOKOHAMA.** | | |
| Via Cape Horn............................. | 20,227 | 11,590 |
| Cape of Good Hope....................... | 18,625 | 9,988 |
| Suez Canal............................... | 17,089 | 8,402 |
| Panama R. R.............................. | 10,611 | 1,974 |
| Isthmus of Tehuantepec................. | 8,637 | ... |
| **NEW ORLEANS TO AUCKLAND, N. Z.** | | |
| Via Suez Canal........................... . | 18,381 | 10,286 |
| Cape of Good Hope....................... | 17,259 | 9,164 |
| Cape Horn................................ | 14,314 | 6,219 |
| Panama R. R.............................. | 9,659 | 1,564 |
| Isthmus of Tehuantepec................. | 8,095 | .... |
| **NEW ORLEANS TO MELBOURNE.** | | |
| Via Suez Canal.............................. | 16,683 | 6,947 , |
| Cape Horn................................ | 15,640 | 5,904 |
| Cape of Good Hope....................... | 15,560 | 5,824 |
| Panama R. R............................... | 11,181 | 1,445 |
| Isthmus of Tehuantepec................. | 9,736 | .... |
| **NEW ORLEANS TO HONOLULU.** | | |
| Via Cape Horn............................. | 16,251 | 10,917 |
| Panama R. R............................... | 7,294 | 1,960 |
| Isthmus of Tehuantepec................. | 5,334 | .... |
| **NEW ORLEANS TO SAN FRANCISCO.** | | |
| Via Cape Horn............................. | 16,112 | 12,551 |
| Panama R. R.............................. | 5,418 | 1,857 |
| Isthmus of Tehuantepec................. | 3,561 | .... |
| **NEW YORK TO VALPARAISO.** | | |
| Via Cape Horn..................... .......... | 10,051 | 8,682 |
| Panama R. R............................. | 5,417 | .... |
| Isthmus of Tehuantepec................. | 6,369 | .... |
| **NEW ORLEANS TO VALPARAISO.** | | |
| Via Cape Horn............................. | 10,476 | 5,436 |
| Panama R. R.............................. | 4,772 | .... |
| Isthmus of Tehuantepec................. | 5,040 | .... |

The total excess of distance over the Tehuantepec Route on these eighteen principal lines is 269,926 miles, or *more than ten times the circumference of the earth.*

Other things being equal commerce will take the shortest lines, whether by steam or sail. The age is seeking for quick despatch in the delivery of all classes of goods. The great saving in distance by the Tehuantepec route is seen at a glance. The cereals of the Pacific coast, which now in their passage to Europe pass around Cape Horn, are nearly five months on the way ; with the Ship Railway, the distance will be shortened nearly eight thousand miles and the time reduced about two and one-half months. This business is very great, and is rapidly increasing, even under the great disadvantages now existing. Reduce the distance and the time one-half, and the producers of the Pacific coast may compete to much better advantage with the producers of India, Australia and other exporting countries. The inevitable result will be that the area of wheat lands will rapidly increase on the Pacific coast ; the exports will double, the farmer will obtain better prices for his productions, and California, Oregon and Washington Territory, no longer separated from the world, will enjoy that prosperity and experience that growth that their fertile soil and delightful climate have a right to expect. The hardy and agricultural immigrant from Europe who, under existing circumstances is barred out from these rich lands by the great expense in reaching them over the transcontinental railroad lines, will, by way of the Tehuantepec route, seek the shores of the Pacific. The whole Atlantic and Gulf coasts of the United States and Mexico will then be able to compete for the trade of Australasia, China and Japan, now passing westward to Europe and New York through the Suez Canal in steamers, or around the Cape of Good Hope in sailing vessels. When it is borne in mind that the commerce of Australasia has increased in the last five years from $225,000,000 to $500,000,-000, and that the United States has now only four per cent. of that trade, the advantage of a direct all-water route can readily be seen. Attention is particularly called to the present most unfortunate position of all the ports of the Gulf of

Mexico, hidden away, as it were, on the further shore of an inland sea, with no exit to the world except in one direction. The trade, to which more than all else, England owes her commercial greatness and her wonderful prosperity in commerce, is the Eastern trade. The trade of the Pacific countries alone is nearly two billion dollars per annum. Consider that the Mississippi Valley and the tributary territory to the ports of the Gulf of Mexico produce every year agricultural, mineral and manufacturing products worth over four billion dollars, and the beneficial results of opening a trade with Asia, Australasia and Polynesia for all the surplus productions of this great valley cannot be grasped by the imagination.

What route could be more favorable than that of Tehuantepec? Then, consider that the whole western coast of South America and Mexico, with a trade even now, via Cape Horn and the Panama Railroad, of about 1,000,000 tons per annum, will be brought by the Ship Railway thousands of miles nearer Vera Cruz, Galveston, New Orleans, New York and other Atlantic ports and Liverpool, and it is at once seen what incentive will be given, not only to trade and commerce, but to productions.

The Tehuantepec route also, will be able to carry much of the heavy freights that now can pass from the Pacific to the Mississippi valley and the Atlantic coast only by expensive railroad transportation, too expensive for the class of goods under consideration. The railways will, however, reap an immense profit from the construction of the Ship Railway by the development of the whole Pacific coast.

It is proper to call attention here to the statement of Lieut. Maury, already given, in reference to the currents and winds in this new highway of commerce. No one will deny his right to teach or attempt to doubt his authority. In the same direction are the statements of Captain Silas Bent, who, before the Merchants' Exchange of St. Louis, pending the unanimous adoption by that body of the resolution recommending a favorable consideration of the ship railway to the United States Government, stated as follows :

" Mere statements of the difference in miles is a very inadequate

" measure of the difference in time that would be occupied by sailing
" vessels in making these several passages, and when we consider that
" three-fourths of the ocean commerce of the world is carried in sail-
" ing vessels, you can see what an important factor this question of
" *sailing-time* becomes in the solution of the problem before us.

" The northeast trade winds which extend across the Atlantic are
" so broken and interrupted when they encounter the West India Isl-
" ands, that they never penetrate the Caribbean Sea ; but the north-
" west portion of them, however, do extend into the Gulf of Mexico,
" and often so far down as to reach well toward Tehuantepec, so that
" whilst in the Gulf winds are always found, yet the Caribbean Sea
" remains a region of almost relentless calm.

" Nor is this all, for the mountain ranges, extending the length of
" the Isthmus of Panama and through Central America, offer a still
" more formidable barrier to the passage of these winds, thus throw-
" ing them still higher into the upper regions of the atmosphere, and
" extending these calms far out into the Pacific Ocean, on the parallel
" of Panama, with lessening width, for fifteen or eighteen hundred
" miles to the northwest, along the coast of Central America.

" This whole region of calms, both in the Caribbean Sea and in the
" Pacific Ocean, is so well known to navigators that sailing vessels
" always shun it, if possible, though they may have to run a thousand
' miles out of their way to do so.

" This absence of wind of course leaves this vast area exposed to
" the unmitigated heat of a torrid sun, except when relieved momen-
" tarily by harassing squalls in the dry season, and by the deluging
" rainfalls of the wet season. With these meterological facts in view,
" let us now suppose that the Lesseps Canal at Panama, and the Eads
" Railway at Tehuantepec are both completed and in running order ;
" then let us start two sailing ships, of equal tonnage and equal speed
" from the mouth of the Mississippi, with cargo for China, one to go
" by the way.of the Panama Canal, and the other by the way of the
" Tehuantepec Railway, and I venture to affirm that by the time the
" Panama vessel has cleared the canal and floats in the waters of the
" Pacific, the Tehuantepec vessel will have scaled the Isthmus and
" be well on to the meridian of the Sandwich Islands ; and that be-
" fore the former vessel can worry through the fifteen or more hun-
" dred miles of windless ocean before her, to reach the trade winds
" to the westward of Tehuantepec, the latter will have sped five thou-
" sand miles on her way across the Pacific, and be fully thirty days
" ahead of her adversary. For it is a fact worth mentioning here,

" that the strength of the northeast trade winds in the Pacific, as well
" as the maximum strength of the northern portion of the great equa-
" torial current in that ocean, are both found on or near the parallel
" of latitude of Tehuantepec, the former blowing with an impelling
" force to the westward of ten or twelve miles an hour, and the latter
" with a following strength of three or four miles per hour."

From the facts and statements advanced, and from the general opinion of·navigators, we are bold to say that the Tehuantepec route not only greatly reduces the distances of all
the present steamer and sailing lines, but is in every way preferable to any other contemplated route in respect to winds
and currents, and in being so near to the commerce and productions of the vast and rapidly growing country lying between the Atlantic and Pacific.

The Senate Committee previously referred to, in the following unequivocal language, not only gave their opinion in favor
of the Tehuantepec route, but supported this opinion by that
given by the Committee of the House óf Representatives.

"During the third session of the 46th Cóngress a special
committee of the House of Representatives charged with the
duty of considering all questions relating to the Isthmus
transit, after an exhaustive investigation reported in favor of
Mr. Eads' Ship Railway project, and selected Tehuantepec as
by all means the most preferable route for the transit-way."
That portion of the report of the House Committee referred
to above, is as follows :

" Mr. Eads has selected the Isthmus of Tehuantepec, and your
" Committee unhesitatingly finds and reports that, of all the routes
" across the isthmus, Tehuantepec is essentially the American route.
" A glance at the map will at once demonstrate the correctness of
" this assertion. If a vessel leaving the mouth of the Mississippi
" river, bound for California ór the Orient, cross the isthmus at
" Tehuantepec, her voyage will be 1250 miles shorter in distance
" than if she crossed at Nicaragua, and 2,200 miles shorter than if
" she crossed at Panama. If a vessel leaving New York, bound for
" the same destination, cross the Isthmus of Tehuantepec, her voy-
" age will be 750 miles shorter than if she went by Nicaragua, and
" 1,250 miles shorter than if she went by Panama. Inasmuch as this
" large saving of distance chiefly affects only the commerce of this

" country and that of Mexico, and not the commerce of Europe, it
" must be at once apparent that the location of a transit way at
" Tehuantepec is of vital importance to the commercial interests of
" the United States.

" The saving of distance is synonymous with cheap transportation.
" Both at Panama and Nicaragua, at various periods throughout the
" year, calms prevail to an extent which would greatly decrease the
" value of either of the routes for sailing vessels. Such, however, is not
" the case at Tehuantepec, as favorable winds always prevail there,
" thus affording a guarantee of no serious detention to sailing
" vessels seeking a passage by that route."

The advantage also of the Ship Railway is seen when we
compare its cost with any sea level canal or canal with locks
that has been projected. The surveys that have been made,
already referred to, the plans of the harbors, all of which
have been carefully considered ; the details of the mechanical
work which have been fully prepared, show that an estimate
of $50,000,000 in cash, is ample to complete and fully equip
the Ship Railway. The maintenance of the works, considering
the substantial character of the construction will be inexpen-
sive. The cost of hauling ships over this railway will be no
more than that of towing and protecting steamers and sailing
vessels through a narrow canal. The speed of vessels through
the canal at Panama will not be more than from two and one-
half to three miles per hour—on the railway ten miles per
hour can be attained—eighteen hours is ample time from
ocean to ocean. It is confidently believed that the cost of
operating will be so much reduced, with no freight to be
handled, no large clerical force to be employed, no great
number of train hands and other employees required as on
ordinary railroads, and the cost of maintenance so small,
that the Ship Railway can carry its freights for from thirty-
five to forty per cent. of its gross receipts. The advantages
in this respect are very fully stated in the following extracts
from a letter of General G. T. Beauregard :

" With regard to the economy of such a ship railway, I would re-
" mark that the tonnage carried over it being moved entirely by
" machinery, and the ratio of paying cargo to dead weight being
" much greater than on ordinary railroads, the cost of operating

" such a railway must be much less. The cost of maintenance should
" also be less in proportion, for the road would be substantially built
" and short in comparison to the amount of tonnage carried over it.
" Moreover the machinery used should be simple and substantially
" made. It is, therefore, safe to assume that the current expenses
" and those of maintenance would not exceed fifty per cent. of the
" gross receipts, which would be more profitable than from a canal
" costing probably two or three times more than a ship railway, and
" three or four times longer to build, thereby increasing greatly the
" amount of interest alone on the actual cost of the canal."

The advantages secured for this route by the liberality of
the Republic of Mexico, which takes a great interest in the
construction of this important work on her territory, is seen
in the favorable terms of the concession granted to Mr. Eads
by that republic. Briefly, they are as follows :—

The right to construct a ship railway, an ordinary railway
and a line of telegraph ; to occupy a right of way about one-
quarter of a mile in width ; a free right of way on public
lands; exemption from all duties on ships, passengers and merchandise in transit ; importation free of duty of all materials
required for construction or maintenance of the railway; exemption from all taxes or other contributions on capital stock
and all property of the company ; a grant of 1,000,000 acres
of public lands ; a guarantee of protection by the use, if
necessary, of naval and military forces without expense to the
company.

In concluding this important part of the subject, it should
be remembered that this route is especially *American*, that
its realization will inevitably result in the exaltation of
the Republic of the United States of the North and
of the Republic of the United States of Mexico, and
that this new tie between these sister republics will
serve to bind them together in stronger bonds. The
great changes which the Ship Railway will bring to both
countries is an important supplement to those benefits
which both have reaped and will continue to reap from the
construction of railways throughout all their vast extent. Pen
cannot decribe ; tongue fails to tell ; none but a prophet
gifted with a vision of the great future could draw the

picture of the western world fifty years from now, with this, the last of the commercial barriers forever broken down.

## FOURTH.

### BUSINESS AND REVENUE.

It is proposed, in treating this subject, to give a fair and reliable statement of the commerce that will either be diverted from the present lines or be developed from altogether new sources of trade. To fully appreciate and understand the results to be stated, an intimate knowledge is requisite of the sources of trade, of the supply and demand, of the handling of different varieties of products of agriculture, manufactures and the mines ; of the distance now traversed by the trade of one country with another ; of the kind and amount of productions and the trade of each country ; the reasons for the trade of, and with, certain countries increasing or decreasing; and many other facts and conditions that affect the commerce of the world.

It would be out of place here to enumerate the great number of details that go to make up the general items of the commercial estimate. A few only are mentioned to familiarize the reader with the subject, and to show that, even under all the disadvantages now existing, there is a foundation on which a substantial and important commerce may be built by the operation of the Tehuantepec Ship Railway. The United States has a feeble commerce with the United States of Colombia on the west coast of South America, carried on either over the Panama Railroad or around Cape Horn. It imports from that country, coffee, barks, hides and india rubber, and exports to it iron, steel, machinery, lard, cotton goods, flour, paper, etc. With Peru, it has a trade in soda and guano, and exports to it cereals, machinery, woods, crude and mineral oil. Strange to say, on account of the difficulties in trading at present with this country, many of the articles are shipped from Peru to France on French steamers, and then re-shipped to New York. We have a similar trade with Chili. Our China trade, either across the Continent by rail, or by the

Panama Railroad, Cape Horn, Cape Good Hope or Suez Canal, is imports of tea, silk, rice, palm-leaf, jute and hemp and exports of cotton cloth, mineral oil, etc. We have about the same character of trade with Hong Kong and Japan. With Australasia we have the foundations of a diversified trade to be built up when the ship railway is completed. The principal imports from that country to the Atlantic coasts of the United States are gums, tins, coal and wool. The principal exports are locomotives, machinery, iron manufactures, household furniture, agricultural implements, illuminating oils, barley, carriages, trunks, sewing machines, linen and cotton goods, books, etc., etc. The most important manufactures exported to that country are twenty-seven in number :

The various groups of islands in Polynesia have a trade that will become important. There is now, with the Sandwich Islands alone, a commerce of over $6,000,000. We receive from them brown sugar, rice and limes, and send them the same general class of goods that go to Australasia.

In 1879 an estimate was made by Joseph Nimmo, Jr., Chief of the Bureau of Statistics, of the commerce that might have crossed the Isthmus in that year (distance alone considered). His estimate was about 3,000,000 tons. In estimating for 1889, ten years after, it is important to note very marked changes and an increase in commerce ; to estimate for Tehuantepec instead of Panama, and to include new business to be developed, which was not then taken into consideration. A notable advance has been made in the trade of the Pacific coast with foreign countries east of Cape Horn. The estimate of 1879 was 551,929 tons. The amount actually exported and imported in 1882 was, including 900,000 tons of cereals and other exports and imports, 1,423,737 tons. This increase, be it remembered, took place even under the extraordinary obstacles and disadvantages that existed, and is the business around Cape Horn alone, and does not include any transcontinental or Panama Railway business. The commerce between the Pacific and Atlantic ports of the United States has nearly doubled in five years. Again, in 1882 the earnings of the grain fleet of the Pacific Coast with Europe was over $15,000,000, and the earnings from the through freights between San Francisco and New York over the transcontinental railroad lines was more than this sum. We may conclude that the tonnage of the latter is larger also, or say 1,500,000 tons. The increase with the opening of the Northern Pacific and Atlantic and Pacific Railroads since then, and from other causes has been very great. The bulky and non-paying of the above freights will probably be diverted to the Ship Railway. Again, on account of the impracticability of sailing vessels navigating the Suez Canal route, about twenty-five per cent. of the business between the United Kingdom and the East Indies is still carried on by sailing vessels around the Cape of Good Hope. As the winds and currents are favorable for sailing vessels via Tehuantepec, and as the distance from many points to Europe is shorter by this line than by the Cape of Good Hope, a certain part of the 800,000 tons now going by that route will probably pass over the Ship Railway. Attention is now particularly called to the entirely new trade which will result from the commercial extension of the Mississippi River into the Pacific Ocean, and the union of the shore lines of the Gulf and the Pacific. Consider that the Mississippi River has an aggregate length of trunk and branches of 165,000 miles ; that it has forty-two navigable tributaries, that many of these tributaries, and the main Mississippi itself is paralleled by prosperous lines of railroad ; that the six trunk lines terminating at New Orleans aggregate 12,559 miles ; that the annual internal commerce of this great valley aggregates nearly $4,000,000,000 ; that the import and export trade of the Pacific countries, Asia and the islands of the Pacific amounts to $2,000.000,000 ; that the cities of the United States, Mexico and the Antilles on the Gulf will fall legitimate heirs to this trade and the interchange of the immense surplus productions ; and we may certainly consider 1,000,000 tons as an item of our estimate for Vera Cruz, Galveston, New Orleans and other Gulf ports, and Havana. The various items made up from reliable sources give an estimate for the Ship Railway business in 1889, of 7,564,597 tons, the details of which are given in the following table :

## DETAILED STATEMENT OF TONNAGE EXPECTED
## OVER THE SHIP RAILWAY,

# In 1889.

| ROUTES BY WHICH COMMERCE MOVES. | Tons 1883. Actual Tonnage carried by steam and sail on routes longer than via Tehuantepec. | Tons 1889. Estimated from ratio of increase of commerce on the routes from 1879 to 1883, and from new business to be developed. |
|---|---|---|
| 1. Panama Railroad...................... | 77,958 | 60,000 |
| 2. U. S. Pacific Coast with Atlantic via Cape Horn........................ | 237,341 | 359,081 |
| 3. Atlantic Ports with Countries west of Cape Horn........................ | 349,454 | 489,135 |
| 4. U. S. Pacific Coast with foreign countries east of Cape Horn............. | 1,423,737 | 2,135,605 |
| 5. European Countries with Countries west of Cape Horn, other than U. S...... | 1,828,621 | 2,285,776 |
| 6. British Columbia (Pacific Coast) with Europe........................... | 125,000 | 235,000 |
| 7. Slow bulky freights now going over Transcontinental lines.............. | 400,000 | 600,000 |
| 8. Fifty per cent. of tonnage now going from Asiatic Countries to Europe via Cape of Good Hope................ | 400,000 | 400,000 |
| 9. New trade to be developed by Ship Railway between Gulf Ports of U. S. and Mexico and Pacific Ocean....... | .... | 1,000,000 |
| Total, | 4,842,111 | 7,564,597 |

The Paris Inter-oceanic Canal Congress, held in 1879, estimated 7,250,000 tons as the tonnage in 1889.

Assuming 6,000,000 tons as a perfectly safe estimate, the annual gross receipts, at $3.00 per ton, will be $18,000,000. Deducting forty per cent. for operating expenses, there remains $10,800,000 of profit to be applied to the payment of interest and dividends, equal to ten per cent. on $108,000,000. A generous estimate for bonds and stock for the construction of the Ship Railway will not exceed $75,000,000. The net profit of $10,800,000 will give an annual return on this amount of about 14½ per cent.

A tax of $2.00 per ton would yield a net profit of $7,200,-000, equivalent to 9 6-10 per cent. on $75,000,000, or 5 per cent. on $144,000,000.

No one who has watched the development of trade and commerce on all lines, by rail or water, will doubt for a moment that a rapid increase of business will take place over the Ship Railway. No more convincing argument, or one more concisely stated, could be given than in the summary of the Suez Canal history by Prof. J. E. Nourse, U. S. N., who has, this year (1884), published an intensely interesting, instructive and complete record of the Suez Canal, and from which we can take a precedent and learn a valuable lesson for the development of business over the Ship Railway :

" First blow struck, 1859. The Mediterranean admitted to ;" Lake Timsah in 1862. Transport of a small vessel, 1865. " Inauguration of the canal, 1869. The estimated tonnage of " 6,000,000 tons reached, 1884. A new canal demanded. De- " cision to double the width of the present canal. Revenue, " 1870 to 1874 (three years), $6,112,129. Revenue for the " *one* year, 1883, $13,702,413. Expectation of $10,000,000 in " 1888 is reported by the British directors. Dividend, 1882, " 17 per cent ; dividend expected in 1890, **30 per cent.**"

As has been shown before, the possibilities and probabilities for a great commerce over the Ship Railway compare favorably with the Suez Canal. It is not too much to say that when this route has been opened a few years, an epitomized record and prophecy may be given that will compare favorably with the above.

We have now covered very briefly (for the importance of the subject,) the commercial necessities, the practicability, the advantages, the business and the revenue of the Tehuantepec Ship Railway.

A thoughtful consideration of this important subject by the people of the United States and Mexico is earnestly requested.

In a broader sense it may be said that the construction of the Tehuantepec Ship Railway will be productive of beneficial results of transcendent importance to the nations.

On this bridge of the world's commerce and civilization the Orient and the Occident will clasp hands in fraternal and perpetual union.

www.ingramcontent.com/pod-product-compliance
Lightning Source LLC
Chambersburg PA
CBHW021445090426
42739CB00009B/1650